WHO AM I?

By Jorgi Owers
Illustrated by Cassandra Bynder

We respect and honour Aboriginal and Torres Strait Islander Elders past, present and future. We acknowledge the stories, traditions and living cultures of Aboriginal and Torres Strait Islander peoples on this land and commit to building a brighter future together.

Library For All Ltd.

I have known I was Aboriginal my whole life. But I looked different from other members of my family. They were dark-skinned and I was fair-skinned.

I grew up mostly in the city, not on my Country. I knew parts of my culture, but not a lot.

At school, we had Indigenous cultural days, and I was expected to know things about my culture. I got nervous. I didn't feel as Aboriginal as the others because of how I looked.

Then, one day, I had the opportunity to attend a cultural camp. I was hoping I would find out more about my culture.

As we sat by the fire with the students from other schools, we listened to the Elders introduce themselves and tell stories.

That was when someone asked me about my culture. I froze. My whole body went cold.

I didn't know what to say. I knew where my mob was from, but that's all I could think of.

I didn't know about my culture. I didn't know where to find it.

At the camp, we learned traditional ways of cooking, weaving, art and storytelling.

I realised that a few people felt the same way I did.

The Elders suggested we go on a journey to discover our culture and learn from our Elders.

"Go back to your Country and connect with Mother Earth," they said. "Culture is taught and learned. The seeds of the spirit of the land already live inside you. It's what connects you to nature and your Country."

So I packed my bags and went searching for it.

I searched high and low, near and far.

I travelled to the ocean and swam for miles, looking. I even asked a school of fish if they had heard about my culture.

Nobody knew.

I walked to the outback and tried talking to the native animals. I came across a kangaroo and asked, "Do you know where my culture is?"

The kangaroo said, "No."

I even walked back to my Country, Kamilaroi land, where I found Elders sitting quietly under a tree listening to the sounds of the earth and connecting deeply and spiritually to our Country.

I sat with them and asked if they knew where I could find my culture.

They looked at me and smiled. They embraced me with a hug, as if to say, welcome home child.

"Child, go and sit over there under the Elder tree. Close your eyes and use your senses to connect your spirit to the Country there. You will soon know."

The silence filled my ears as I walked
to the spot.

I went and sat by myself on the land,
and I wondered, *Where could it be?*

As I became quiet and still, something inside me awakened.

I could feel the beat of Mother Earth matching the beat of my heart. I could hear the songs of the birds fill my soul with joy.

I felt connected spiritually to the land and felt like I was home, full and peaceful at the same time. I could feel my ancestors welcoming me.

It was then that I realised that my culture was inside me, and always had been. It wasn't the knowledge I was taught or the colour of my skin.

It was my spirit.

It was the core of my being.

I joined the Elders back in their circle and we spoke so many words without a single voice being heard. The spirit of the trees and earth connected us all harmoniously.

I felt free. I felt at home. Now I felt like I knew my culture, and it was alive inside of me.

You can use these questions to talk about this book with your family, friends and teachers.

What did you learn from this book?

Describe this book in one word. Funny? Scary? Colourful? Interesting?

How did this book make you feel when you finished reading it?

What was your favourite part of this book?

Download the Library For All Reader app from librariyforall.org

About the contributors

Jorgi Owers is a Kamilaroi woman from Gumedah, now living in Meringandan, Queensland. She loves to yarn with her family over a home-cooked meal. Her favourite story as a child was about Barbie Mermaidia.

Cassandra Bynder is a Ballardong-Whadjuk Noongar woman raised in the south west of Western Australia on Wadandi Noongar Country. She loves taking long coastal hikes with her kids and teaching art skills to the community. One of her favourite books when she was little was the *Faraway Tree* series by Enid Blyton.

Author's Country

Darwin

NORTHERN
TERRITORY

QUEENSLAND

WESTERN
AUSTRALIA

SOUTH
AUSTRALIA

Brisbane

NEW SOUTH
WALES

OUR YARNING

Perth

Adelaide

ACT

Sydney

Canberra

VICTORIA

Melbourne

Illustrator's Country

TASMANIA
Hobart

Our Yarning

The Our Yarning collection aligns with the Australian Curriculum through the Cross-Curriculum Priorities — Aboriginal and Torres Strait Islander Histories and Cultures. The collection provides an authentic opportunity for learning and embedding Aboriginal and Torres Strait Islander perspectives because it is written by Aboriginal and Torres Strait Islander people.

We know that children learn better, and enjoy reading more, when they see themselves in the stories, characters and illustrations of the books they read.

To download the app, visit the Google Play Store or Apple Store and search 'Our Yarning'.

libraryforall.org

You're reading Upper Primary

Learner – Beginner readers

Start your reading journey with short words, big ideas and plenty of pictures.

Level 1 – Rising readers

Raise your reading level with more words, simple sentences and exciting images.

Level 2 – Eager readers

Enjoy your reading time with familiar words, but complex sentences.

Level 3 – Progressing readers

Develop your reading skills with creative stories and some challenging vocabulary.

Level 4 – Fluent readers

Step up your reading skills with playful narratives, new words and fun facts.

Middle Primary – Curious readers

Discover your world through science and stories.

Upper Primary – Adventurous readers

Explore your world through science and stories.

Who Am I?

First published 2024

Published by Library For All Ltd
Email: info@libraryforall.org
URL: libraryforall.org

This book was created in collaboration with Yalari to improve and support the educational outcomes of First Nations children in Australia. We thank Yalari for their ongoing support of the Our Yarning program.

Educating Indigenous Children

Our Yarning logo design by Jason Lee, Bidjipidji Art

Original illustrations by Cassandra Bynder

Who Am I?
Owers, Jorgi
ISBN: 978-1-923207-61-5
SKU04422